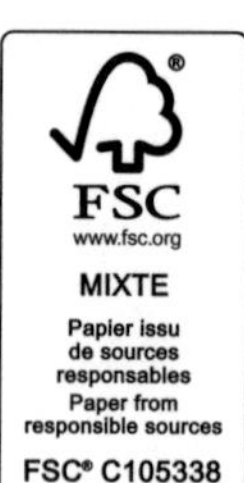

Edition : Books on Demand,
12/14 rond-Point des Champs-Elysées, 75008 Paris
Impression : BoD - Books on Demand, Norderstedt, Allemagne
ISBN : 9782322118540
Dépôt légal : Septembre 2019

NORAH CUSTAUD

Painters
in the Garden of Gethsemane

PAINTERS

IN THE GARDEN OF GETHSEMANE

Each painting mysteriously holds an entire
life, with all its suffering,
its doubts, its exuberance and light.[1]

Introduction

The different representations of the story of Jesus Christ on the Mount of Olives create lasting images of an important episode in the history of humanity: the incarnation of Christ, who experienced being human and all its attendant suffering: "Just as there was, there is and there will be no man whose nature has been assumed by Our Lord Jesus Christ, there was and there will be no man for whom he has not suffered ".[2]

Firstly, this work underlines the originality of the story which has given rise to many visual representations over the years. It shows how the Gethsemane story has inspired numerous artists and what they have individually contributed to our understanding of Jesus' abandonment. Secondly, it offers a deeper analysis of the works of two painters, Gauguin (1848-1903) and Rembrandt (1606-1669), and their interpretations of the Gethsemane drama which were influenced by their personal experiences of abandonment and loneliness. What did they learn from this Gospel account in which Jesus, in his prayers, reveals his angst at being abandoned on the Mount of Olives?

Multiple readings allow us to sense the greatness of God's love which is at the heart of the story. This love is the root of all faith, a source of comfort and the foundation for hope that man can carry throughout the 21st century.

I

Representations of Jesus in the Garden of Gethsemane

Representations of Jesus in the Garden of Gethsemane

The story of Jesus in Gethsemane has influenced painting since the beginning in the 15th century, notably. It has inspired artists as diverse as Dürer, Mantegna, El Greco, Blake and Bellini. Some works are distinguished by their originality like those of Gauguin, who represented Christ in the Garden of Gethsemane in his own likeness, or Rembrandt's lithographs. Many contemporary artists continue to reference passages in the Bible, painting them in their own way, like the Chinese painter He Qi with his colourful style and Chinese folk-art[3] inspired forms as well as the versatile American painter Anthony Falbo, whose works of art have been influenced by Rembrandt's use of light and shadow and the Cubism of Picasso. Anthony Falbo has created several remarkable religious works in the Cubist style such as *Gethsemane The Hour is Near*[4].

We have specifically chosen to analyze different representations of Jesus in the Garden of Gethsemane since the artists' work enriches our study of the biblical story through their depictions of the characters as well as their light and shadow effects.

Their representations can help us read the Bible at a deeper level by presenting us with different perspectives. As such, they offer new interpretations of the biblical story because they are not merely simple illustrations but rather, personal reflections and imaginative conceptions.

In addition, interpretations in the form of images create an exciting opportunity to renew theological language. When looking at the gestures or expressions of the different characters represented (Jesus, the disciples or the angel) and simultaneously feeling the emotions that they evoke, we realize once again that these individuals are not imaginary; we recognize that they were once present in our world, living as incarnated beings, with feelings just like us. As for the diversity of representations, they encourage us to thoughtfully reflect on

Christ's incarnation in the context of human history, particularly in the Garden of Gethsemane where Jesus suffered both physically and spiritually. Certain artists who have had a particular attraction to the Scriptures have tried to explore these texts but more often than not what interests them is representing Jesus praying in the Garden of Gethsemane. In fact, the image is a means by which to connect with the Gospel and as it follows, with God.

Bernadette Neipp[5] thinks that the first representations of Jesus, beginning in the 4th century, do not explore or express his weakness. Such is the case with the mosaic from the year 520 in the basilica in Ravenna in which Jesus appears standing in the centre with his arms raised; he almost dominates his disciples who are seated around him, ever attentive. From the 14th century, the Gethsemane drama has been interpreted with a different sensibility: one that recognizes Jesus' suffering and does not shy away the agony and loneliness that he felt while his disciples were sleeping. This interpretation of the Gethsemane drama has since persisted unchanged.

Numerous works represent the agony in three stages. In the foreground, the sleeping disciples, then Jesus, struggling in prayer, and then finally, an interlocutor who takes the form of an angel or God himself. Other artists prefer to juxtapose three smaller scenes in a triptych capturing three distinct moments in Gethsemane. Jesus in prayer, Jesus comforted by an angel and Jesus waking his sleeping disciples.

The Character of Jesus

The Character of Jesus

On the Mount of Olives, Jesus is
sometimes represented far away from his
disciples [6] on higher ground, usually a
mound[7] or hill[8]. Luke describes the distance as being "about a stone's throw"
(Luke 22:41) from the disciples who are
asleep on lower ground. Certain prints such
as those by Dürer represent Jesus occupy-
ing more space in the scene while the sleeping disciples occupy a smaller and less visible space[9]. Choosing the Gospel of Luke,
certain artists represent Jesus on his knees[10]
praying, with his hands clasped or his arms
out stretched. But we can also find him
with his face pressed to the ground[11] according to Mark and Matthew: "he fell with
his face to the ground" (Matthew: 26:39).
Sometimes he is even seated, on the verge
of fainting from fatigue [12]. Luke notes:
"And being in anguish, he prayed more earnestly, and his sweat was like drops of

blood falling to the ground" (Luke 22:44). This detail about the blood-like sweat of Jesus, mentioned only by Luke, has drawn little interest from artists, the exception being the German painter Hans Multscher, who wanted to emphasize the horror of the moment. He represented Jesus praying, his eyes cast towards the heavens, his hands clasped but pointed slightly downwards towards the ground; the drops of blood are visible [13]. In contrast, most artists have sought to elevate Jesus. The Gospel of Mark only mentions him moving away to pray[14], likely to distinguish him from the disciples and show that even in a moment of human weakness, Jesus remained the Son of God and Our Lord. It is also worth mentioning that other interpretations of Jesus such as those by Asian[15], African[16] and Native American painters[17] have not hesitated to incorporate features from their own cultures when painting Jesus.

The Angel Who Offers the Cup or the Cross

The Angel Who Offers the Cup or the Cross

The angel in the Gospel of Luke is frequently represented holding a cup in hand. The idea of the cup, found in the Old Testament, symbolizes a test to be passed. In a number of paintings, there is a host over the cup. According to a non-scriptural reading, this cup anticipates key elements of the Passion: the cross[18], the crown of thorns, the vinegar-soaked sponge on the end of a wooden stick, the pillar where Christ is flagellated and finally, the spear with which the soldiers confirm his death[19]. Two painters, the Italian Lorenzo Ghiberti[20] and the German Albrecht Altdorfer, depicted an angel across from Jesus proffering the host. It seems that Jesus is confronting the inevitable consequences of the gift that he made several hours earlier during the Last Supper: the gift of his body and blood symbolized by bread and wine. Elsewhere, we find angels floating in the heavens or arranged on a cloud presenting the cross[21]. The angel as described in Luke often appears in a corner of the composition making a gesture of blessing[22]; he also comforts Jesus by holding him in his arms[23]: "I long to dwell in your tent forever and take refuge in the shelter of your wings" (Psalms 61:4). At times the angel[24] is replaced by God whose blessed right hand, head or torso can be glimpsed.

In conclusion, the angel frequently appears in such representations. Not surprisingly, given that, during certain periods, this angel was worshipped as a protector, able to keep those who trusted in him away from danger. The painters have thus been particularly responsive to the account given in the Gospel of Luke.

The Disciples

The Disciples

Certain artists represent the disciples[25] together while others prefer to follow the Gospel of Mark and depict only three disciples: Peter, illustrated with a beard and white hair; John, a young man without a beard, and James with a beard and brown hair[26].

Luke is the only one who provides an explanation as to why the disciples are sleeping and that is that their sadness overwhelms them and causes them to fall asleep. They are represented in various ways: sleeping on the ground "Jesus returned and found them sleeping" (Matthew 26:43), sprawled out as we see them in the work of Mantegna (London, 1459). As for Botticelli, he depicted two disciples lying down, extended[27]. In numerous paintings, the apostles are covered by their cloaks[28]. Sometimes the three disciples are uncomfortably placed on rocky ground and seem to be curled up while sleeping or, rather dozing, as we see in the work of Giovanni Bellini[29].

Dürer's work deserves particular attention since he provided a different image of the three sleeping apostles: the oldest, Peter, sleeps with his hand gripping the sword that he will soon use: "With that, one of Jesus' companions reached for his sword, drew it out and struck the servant of the high priest, cutting off his ear" (Matthew 26:51); James, his chin in his hands, seems to be overtaken with nightmares; and John, whose face is marked by worry, seems to be dreaming rather than soundly sleeping[30].

The Soldiers

The Soldiers

It is in the Garden of Gethsemane that Jesus will be arrested by soldiers led by Judas. The arrest is mentioned by Matthew and Mark: "While he was still speaking, Judas, one of the Twelve, arrived. With him was a large crowd armed with swords and clubs" (Mark 14:43, Matthew 26:47). Although the arrest follows Christ's agony in the Garden of Gethsemane, certain paintings anticipate this episode by bringing together the two scenes in a single composition. The Garden of Gethsemane by Andrea Mantegna figures among these paintings. He depicted a long and sinuous route along which Judas leads the soldiers to his master in order to stop him "with torches, lanterns and weapons" (John 18:3).

The painting by artist Hanz Multscher illustrates Judas' brutal manner of entering the garden with soldiers armed with pikes and spears; they burst into the painting, in effect. In another work by Mantegna, five angels perched on a cloud hold a cross, while at the other end, Judas approaches with the soldiers (London, 1455).

Lastly, there is to be discovered a highly original representation of the Mount of Olives at the Notre-Dame Cathedral in Strasbourg. In the 15th century, Veit Wagner sculpted, behind Jesus, a hook-nosed Judas grasping a purse in his hand; this is indeed the money that he received for delivering his master to the high priests who had "promised to give him money".

Judas "watched for an opportunity to hand him over" (Mark 14:10-11). Judas also holds a rope in his hand which signifies his final end. The sculptor added a snake to the scene to symbolize the Evil lurking around Judas as if he, as a traitor, were doomed to Hell. There are soldiers behind Judas, some of them wearing armour and helmets with swords in hand, and others carrying pikes and spears. The presence of Judas and the soldiers in the Gethsemane scene effectively establishes the moment of Jesus' praying as the beginning of the Passion. It is also a way of signifying that at that moment Jesus already knew that his arrest was imminent.

The Garden

The Garden

The Mount of Olives or, Garden of Gethsemane, is located near Jerusalem, on the other side of the Kidron Valley. Certain artists represent the site as an enclosure whose boundaries we can clearly make out[31] while others paint a landscape comprised of hills, rocks and copious, thorny plants. Some painters, like Bellini, envisaged a barren and arid environment with nothing more than a garden[32]. Other modifications to the story of the Agony have been introduced without any apparent basis in the Gospels.

Fra Angelico (Florence, 1440), for example, complemented the scene with Martha and Mary at prayer in their home[33]. In 1840, Janmot emphasized the drama of the event by a pronounced chiaroscuro effect in which the solitary Christ is illuminated by a beam of light [34] . Tissot represented Jesus in a cave surrounded by angels who hold globes illustrating scenes from the Passion, including the veil of Saint Veronica and the Lamentation[35] of the Virgin Mary[36]. The Virgin Mary's suffering is expressed in a poem attributed to the Franciscan monk Jacopone da Todi: "There stood the mother of sorrows in tears at the foot of the cross, on which her son hung dying; Her grieving soul, now shared the painful sadness that pierced it like a sword." (…) Who would not pity the tears of the Mother of Christ, seeing her in such torment? Who would not feel a profound compassion contemplating the Mother of Christ suffering alongside her Son?[37]

It is evident that by representing Jesus in Gethsemane the artists were attempting to communicate a deeper and richer message: they were not only depicting what they learned from the Gospels but also what they felt. The smallest details of Jesus' anguished face, the loneliness, pain and despair evoked by the posture of the sleeping apostles, the way in which the soldiers and the garden itself are represented: all of these elements lend gravity to the Gethsemane scene and create drama in each work. The agony of Jesus, likewise represented, is no longer only understood through a simple reading of the biblical text but instead, a basis for an interpretation that both allows the scene to be richly imagined as well as experienced through emotions of the artists. Moreover, these representations are a universal means of encountering the Gospel since they go beyond linguistic, intellectual, cultural and denominational boundaries.

Such power is readily observable in Gauguin and Rembrandt, two artists who both made a rigorous study of Gethsemane, and let it touch their lives. In a particularly dark period in his life, Gauguin identified with Jesus, abandoned by all on the Mount of Olives.

Gauguin, lonely, suffering and misunderstood, lent his own features to the suffering Jesus dominating the scene in his representation. In contrast, Rembrandt represented a Jesus comforted by an angel who physically holds him up. An analysis of their two works, markedly different due to their historical periods and styles, reveals the unique approach that each artist took in rendering Jesus in the Garden of Gethsemane.

The self-portraits by Gauguin do not only represent the artist himself, abandoned, but also make it possible for the viewer to see him or herself in the protagonist. Rembrandt, gifted at expressing intense emotions, tried in his paintings to appeal to the viewer on an emotional level. He wanted to bring deep emotions up to the surface, such as those that compelled the Father of Jesus when he tried to comfort his Son.

II

Two Painters in the Garden of Gethsemane

Christ on the Mount of Olives

Paul Gauguin

Christ on the Mount of Olives

by Paul Gauguin

Born in Paris in 1848, Paul Gauguin was a post-Impressionist painter[38]. A number of factors influenced his exceptional work *Christ on the Mount of Olives*: his personal life, including his friendships, and his sources. Gauguin rued his difficult experiences and the sadness that his austere life in Paris brought him. He referred to Paris as a "desert for the poor man"[39].

He suffered immensely on account of his material circumstances and the failure of his shows to make an impact on the public. Later, in his memoirs which he dedicated to his daughter Aline, he wrote: "I have known extreme misery, which is to say, hunger and everything that comes from that"[40]. He found inspiration in diverse sources like the paintings of Manet, Japanese prints, ceramics, Cloisonism,

Celtic art and primitive art in general. Gauguin was not religious in the ordinary sense of the word but he was prone to mysticism, and was struck by the sincerity and candour of the faith exhibited by the peasants of Brittany. He felt the pull of popular religion, which was a mixture of faith and superstition.

In 1888, Gauguin began his first religious painting: *Jacob Wrestling with the Angel.* This work marks his definitive break with Impressionism and his movement towards Symbolism. At that time, the artist sought repose in Le Pouldu, Brittany. He had lived earlier in Pont-Aven but, according to him, the town, though favoured by his colleagues, had become "full of strange and abominable people"[41].

It was during the course of his stay here that Gauguin created *Christ on the Mount of Olives*[42], which he painted in November 1889. In this painting, the features of Christ clearly show that it is a self-portrait of the artist. If not convinced, one only has to look at another self-portrait from one year earlier, *Les Miserables*, which the painter created for Van Gogh. This first self-portrait references Victor Hugo's novel by the same name. Gauguin identifies with the character Jean Valjean because like him, he felt persecuted by society. At first glance, the viewer sees a convict, Jean Valjean, but then also the lowly Impressionist painter[43]. Gauguin would not be content to forever represent himself as Jean Valjean. Eventually, he moved on to Christ at a particular moment in the Saviour's life : at Gethsemane when he was betrayed by Judas and forsaken by his sleeping apostles.

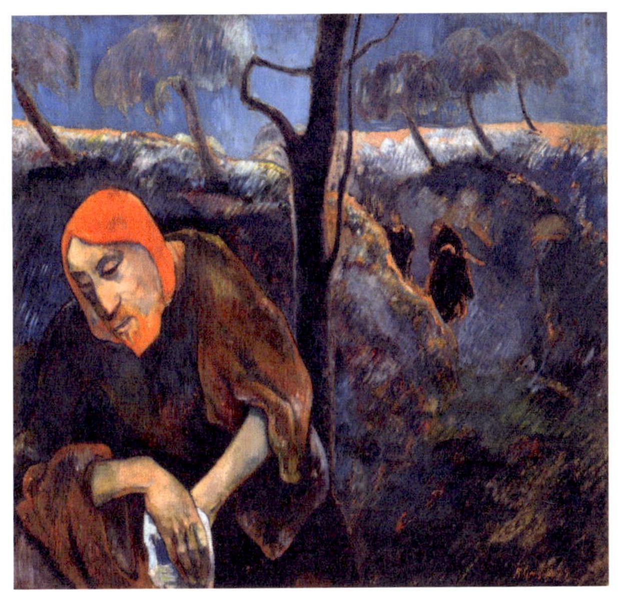

PAUL GAUGUIN
Christ on the Mount of Olives, 1889
Oil on canvas
28 1/2 x 36 in (72.4 x 91.4 cm)
Norton Museum of Art, West Palm
Beach, Florida,
Gift of Elizabeth C. Norton, 46.5

During its creation, Gauguin considered the painting his best work: "I think that I have just created my best work. A Christ on the Mount of Olives"[44]. The painter portrayed himself as a person misunderstood, humiliated, forced to work, impoverished and tortured, and who felt abandoned by some and betrayed by others.

Considering this painting, one detail in particular stands out: this self-portrait is not painted as if it were a likeness seen in a mirror. Gauguin represented Christ with a hooked nose and his eyes lowered, and placed him in the left lower corner of the painting, emphasizing his humility and sorrow. Interestingly, the artist painted a path leading to the Mount of Olives resembling the typical sunken lanes of Brittany in Gauguin's time. Furthermore, the tree line in the background follows the curvature of palm trees although they are apple trees. This manner of painting is more symbolic than realistic. It is most certainly not purely figurative. As Gauguin wrote to Schuffenecker in 1888: "Art is an abstraction. Bring your art forth by dreaming in its presence and think more of the creation which will result. The only way to ascend to God is to create like our Divine Master"[45].

Christ has red hair, a symbol of his human suffering. This reminds of the Gospel of Luke; "And being in anguish, he prayed more earnestly, and his sweat was like drops of blood falling to the ground" (Luke 22:44). Jesus' posture does not accord with what is described in the Gospels or what other painters had depicted. Gauguin's Christ is seated, almost slumping, with his hands crossed, expressing his pain and resignation.

In the background, three small figures are fleeing behind a ravine. One might think that these are the disciples that betrayed him. It should be noted that the Gethsemane story does not mention the flight of the disciples, but only their sleep. It seems that Gauguin was inspired here by the German painter Dürer and his series of woodcuts collectively entitled *Small Passion*, created in 1511.

This hypothesis is based on the fact that Dürer had already represented Christ alone and tortured in a similar position, although he had depicted Him with the marks of stigmata and wearing a crown of thorns. It is in this manner that Gauguin wanted to imagine the saviour of the world.

In fact, Gauguin dreamed of unity among men to be brought about through the propagation of culture and universal truth. He saw Christianity and democracy as being aligned, as exemplified by Christ's principle that all men are brothers and that "whoever wants to be first must be the slave of all" (Mark 10:45). Such systems of thought - Christian brotherhood and modern democracy under which free citizens are subject to the same law of equality - lay the groundwork for kinship and understanding, conditioning us to avoid dissidence and conflict. In this way, Christianity and democracy do seem to complement each other, do they not?[46]

It was through his artistic works that Gauguin tried to express his personal conception of the world and life. He wanted to show others his vision of things and present himself as a new prophet, a saviour of the world, and, at the same time, express what was inside him: anxious desires and, in a word, anguish. Gauguin, an artist who rebelled against the intellectual and social norms of his time, was rejected, banished and abandoned by his contemporaries.

The Agony in the Garden
Rembrandt Van Rijn

The Agony in the Garden
by Rembrandt Van Rijn

Rembrandt was one of the rare artists to have illustrated as many stories from the Old Testament as the New Testament. It seems that he was inspired by the emerging desire to represent the transcendent in the human world in works in which he skillfully used chiaroscuro. He was an artist who translated biblical stories with a sense of gravity and much theological detail, as seen in his representation of Gethsemane. His interpretation of the drama of Jesus in the Garden of Gethsemane is in fact one of the most original engravings of his time.

Rembrandt, a faithful believer and dedicated reader of the Bible, always sought to illustrate biblical passages in a personal way in order to uncover new meanings that were both unique and universally understandable. He is known for having been able to impart human feeling to his portraits and religious scenes. His main religious works are *Disciples at Emmaüs* (1648), *The Sacrifice of Isaac* (1655) and *The Agony in the Garden* (1657). The strong emotions elicited by these works seem to reflect the deep feelings of the artist himself as evidenced by the painting *Disciples at Emmaüs*: "The figure of Christ is above all else admirable, his pale face radiant, his lips half-open and his eyes, having seen death, large and glassy, while his whole person is exuding compassion and authority!"[47].

In 1657, the painter went through a difficult period. He ran into trouble with his creditors and had to sell everything. At the age of 52, he found himself without a home or means: "he felt abandoned by his contemporaries (…) at that moment in his life the future seemed undoubtedly dark to him. But like precious metals in the furnace that only give the fire the impurities with which they are mixed in a process of becoming more precious still, the genius of the master would continue to be perfected and expanded in the face of misfortune"[48]. He was thus compelled to take up his work again. He chose a religious theme to render in an engraving, that of Christ on the Mount of Olives. This work manages to "reach out and touch the eyes and heart of the viewer so much so that even in its materiality it is spiritual in the same way that Maritain said that poetry is the spiritual inscribed on and expressed through the sensible"[49]. In this engraving, the painter used the aquatint technique[50] that he had already employed in other scenes from the life of Jesus. Small in size[51], this engraving is housed today in the National Gallery of Canada.

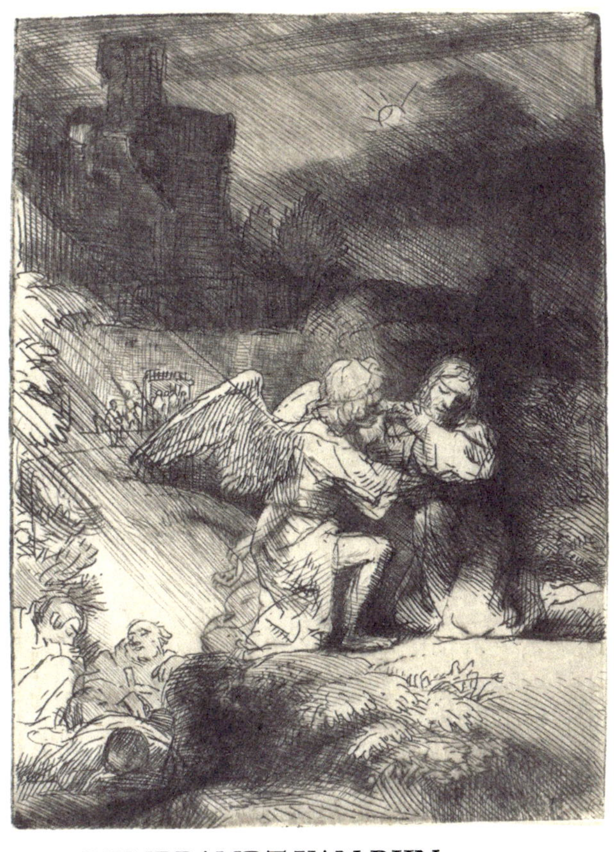

REMBRANDT VAN RIJN
The Agony in the Garden, v.1657.
Aquatint and drypoint on laid paper,
11.1 x 8.4 cm
National Gallery of Canada, Ottawa

Rembrandt chose the version of the Gethsemane story told in the Gospel of Luke and represented a faltering Christ supported by an angel, his apostles deep in sleep beside him. In his interpretation the artist used chiaroscuro with great subtlety. This method is based on the opposition between parts that are illuminated in a scene and those that are plunged into darkness: "chiaroscuro in Rembrandt is never a juxtaposition but a struggle between darkness and light that both forces create (…), that can only produce in the end a dialogue that challenges the viewer"[52]. This technique was not only of aesthetic value to the artist but also of metaphysical and spiritual value. As Pascal said: "If there were no darkness, men would not feel their depravity; if there were no light, men would not hope for their salvation. And so, it is not only right, but helpful to us, that God is partially hidden, and partially revealed"[53].

In the foreground are the two main characters that are placed on a mound. Here, Rembrandt continued the artistic tradition of representing variations in terrain. The mountain was a place of prayer where

Jesus spoke to his Father: "Jesus took Peter, John and James with him and went up onto a mountain to pray" (Luke 9:28, 6:12).

The characters are not drawn with the same scale. Jesus and the angel are taller than the three disciples asleep down to the left of the etching. In the background, there is a dark landscape with a tower barely lit by the faint glimmers of the moon and, beneath the tower, characters with indiscernible features. How the contrast has been executed demands attention. While some details, like the characters of the angel and Jesus, are finished with minute care, others, like the soldiers, are barely outlined. These choices manifest the deep feelings of the artist.

In terms of lighting, Rembrandt used light to highlight the important moments in the scene. As Joachim von Sandrat said about the master's paintings: "There is little light in his works, except for the places where he wanted to concentrate interest; elsewhere, he brought together with great skill and in perfect measure light and shadow and deftly illustrated darkness creeping in; his colouring was strong and everything revealed a clear vision"[54]. Here, only two characters are illuminated, while

the rest of the space is plunged into darkness. Rembrandt cast rays of light on the
kneeling characters in the centre and even
on the sleeping disciples to intensify the
dramatic effect of the scene and direct the
viewer's attention to the characters' states
of mind.

Light is quite present here: "the
light of God, it lights all men coming into
the world"[55]. The divine light comes from
outside the image with the appearance of
the angel rather than from the moon which
emits only weak light: "But in those days,
following that distress, the sun will be dark-
ened, and the moon will not give its light"
(Mark 13:24). The luminosity demonstrates
that the work is the artist's personal reading since the account in the Gospel of Luke
mentions the angel but not any particular
light. It is pure imagination on Rembrandt's part who interpreted Gethsemane
in a new way. He added a bright light en-
veloping Jesus and the angel as well as the
disciples. For the painter, this burst of light
in the dark night of Gethsemane symbolized the presence of God who often comes
to shed light for us when our lives are dark-
ened by difficulties and our weaknesses.

As a result, Rembrandt was insisting that God never abandons us in our distress. On the contrary, God penetrates the core of our suffering and comforts us as he comforted his Son by sending him his angel: "for me light is one with you Lord; it transcends and is your resurrection even in the darkest night in the Garden of Gethsemane"[56].

The posture of the angel supporting Jesus in close contact recalls another engraving by Rembrandt that he created two years earlier around 1655: *The Sacrifice of Isaac* in which the angel holds the hand of Abraham. In these two aquatints, what is striking is the posture of the characters rather than their faces. In the engraving of Gethsemane, the angel stands in front of Jesus, his face in shadows; his way of leaning on his right leg shows that he is trying to lift Jesus up or at least support him. The light only illuminates one half of Jesus' body while the other remains in darkness. Jesus turns his head slightly so that the viewer can better see his face. He is on his knees, a position emphasizing the humility of Jesus before the Father, even at the height of his anguish. He has his hands clasped and his eyes closed, which shows that he is praying hoping that he will not have to take up his cup; however, Rembrandt gave the impression that the angel is the answer to this prayer of Jesus.

It is true that the Gospel of Luke presents Jesus as weak and very human, in need of comfort from an angel sent by the Father: "An angel from heaven appeared to him and strengthened him" (Luke 22:43). Yet the engraving by Rembrandt attempts, through the closeness and physical contact between the two characters, to make visible or emphasize the strength that Jesus received from the angel of God. This strength allowed him to bear the pain of being abandoned by his disciples and confront his destiny.

Looking closely, it is possible to see the three disciples sleeping near one other, in the bottom left corner. As far as this detail is concerned, Rembrandt did not follow the Gospel of Luke, which does not separate the disciples, but rather that of Mark and Matthew who emphasize the three privileged disciples, Peter, James and John: "He took Peter, James and John along with him. And he began to be deeply distressed and troubled." (Mark 14:33, Matthew 26:37). They are represented far away from Jesus, perhaps to contrast the sleep of the disciples with Jesus' deep distress who "at the moment when he needs the people close to him to support him, he sees them sleeping like the dead, numb to the world except that of their dreams"[57].

At the bottom of the etching is a door towards which Judas is moving, leading the group that will seize his master. It is also noticeable that there is significant distance between Jesus and his disciples on one hand, and between him and the soldiers on the other. In this engraving, Rembrandt did not depict sweat transforming into drops of blood, nor the motif of the cup or the cross. It seems that for the artist the simple gesture of the angel was enough to express the silent presence of the Father.

This representation is the work of a believer and reflects his personal responses to questions that haunted him throughout his life. It gives us insight into the intimacy of the connection he had with the One he was looking for. Through some of his works, including that of *The Agony in the Garden*, Rembrandt invites us to face our fears and suffering and to assume them as Christ did in the Garden of Gethsemane. He believed that we are not alone, abandoned to our fate, because God is with us.

He communicated this with a gesture of tenderness: "God quietly inhabits those gestures that touch and make the imagination of the heart real"[58]. The talent of this 17th century Dutch painter lay in his ability to appeal to the emotions: "the greatness of Rembrandt is in having stepped outside of his milieu, having remained true to his genius, and having continued along his path (…), strong in his only conviction, having waited confidently for judgment day[59]". Rembrandt's genius was so original and so sincere that he deserves to be admired by all. To that end, in 1936, Wilhelm Martin wrote: "Rembrandt essentially reflects the best within us: deep religious convictions, a conscience and a spirit of freedom, and an insatiable and indomitable desire to act[60]". During his lifetime Rembrandt executed several works about Jesus in Gethsemane, as if the painter found comfort in representing the deeply human struggle of Jesus. Consequently, Rembrandt continues to touch us and move us today with the originality of his work.

To conclude, a prayer that could have inspired this great painter in his work is presented here for reflection. As Bernadette Neipp says, the following prayer simultaneously expresses the sensitivity and faith inhabiting Rembrandt's very spirit and being:

> "O Christ, I felt very close to you when engraving the scene at Gethsemane. At that moment, you truly experienced suffering as a man alone, so much so that you needed the tender support of the angel who came to your side when you were most vulnerable. What allowed you to intimately understand all living beings on this earth, there, in the Garden of Gethsemane, was your profound humanity. And so, it is through the physical contact with the angel holding you up that I try to express your suffering as a man alone, suffering that would be felt by anyone abandoned by his fellow human beings.
>
> O Christ, in chiaroscuro, I attempt to translate the mystery of salvation that I feel deeply within me. As in all my work, the play of light is essential. For me, light is one with you, Lord; it transcends you and speaks of your resurrection, even in the darkest night in the Garden of Gethsemane.
>
> Through my use of chiaroscuro, I am able to express all the complexity of

the Gospels through the often barely perceptible transitions between night and day, as one gives way to the other.

O Christ, the angel that came to fill your heart with strength speaks to me personally. For me, he could not have been a distant angel, appearing in heaven as you stretched out the cup, as depicted by my great predecessor Dürer and so many others before him. For me, he had to be an unmistakable presence, a presence that you could feel in your whole being, soul, mind and body. Hence this tender support which is my personal interpretation of this moment of the story.

I have felt your presence all through my life through my loved ones. And my works that try to translate your Word tangibly are the most vivid expression of it. This support, both physical and spiritual, has helped me to overcome the sorrows and fears that have punctuated my life, as it will continue to do so for all living beings on this earth[61]."

Conclusion

A study of the representations of Gethsemane by Rembrandt and Gauguin allow us to discover the originality in each artist's work and the differences between them despite being based on the same story. For each of these two painters, the crucial moment on the Mount of Olives had a significant impact on their life.

On one hand, for Rembrandt, it shows that God is always present, even in the depths of suffering. The painter communicated this idea through the tenderness of the angel's gesture and the light pouring in from outside in *The Agony in the Garden*. For him, Jesus is thus neither alone nor abandoned by his Father. Rembrandt's interpretation is not a kind of projection, as it might be in the case of certain romantic poets to be discovered in the second booklet, but rather, the fruit of a meditation on God incarnated as the man Jesus Christ who joined man in all his weakness and suffering. That Jesus accepted to do the will of his Father until his death on the cross.

On the other hand, Gauguin, in painting *Christ on the Mount of Olives*, represented himself as abandoned. He wanted to use the agony of Christ as a point of reference to express and reflect his own inner struggle. As if in the Garden of Gethsemane the suffering of Jesus transcended all men that are alone and feel abandoned by others, or simply by God. This feeling that Gauguin[62] experienced is one that continues to torment men today.

Through his incarnation, Christ suffered in the Garden of Gethsemane as a man and for all men, in their place. He knew fear and silence as he experienced the loneliness felt by all men. This is why no one should feel alienated from the person of Jesus because he identified himself with the destiny of all. Christ is then an example given to men to emulate when confronting

adversity. He accepted death in order to offer humanity a new life, a life that leads the
children of God to love, and not to solitude
and injustice.

Acknowledgements

I want to offer profuse thanks to the American painter Anthony Falbo for graciously granting me the right to use his painting *Gethsemane The Hour is Near* on the cover of this book.

I also want to thank the Norton Museum of Art in West Palm Beach in Florida for having graciously given me authorization to use Paul Gauguin's painting *Christ on the Mount of Olives*.

Thank you again to each person who helped me accomplish this project.

Table of Contents

Notes

---

[1] Wassily Kandinsky, *Concerning the Spiritual in Art and Painting in Particular,* Denoël, 1989, p. 56.

Introduction

[2] Olegario Gonzalez de Cardedal, « Expérience religieuse et création artistique », in Communio, 20, July-August 1995, pp. 145-146.

[3] He Qi, *Praying at Gethsemane*, 1999, China.

[4] Anthony Falbo, *Gethsemane The Hour is Near,* 2006, Florida.

[5] Bernadette Neipp, *Gethsémané, Rembrandt et le dernier combat de Jésus,* Switzerland, 1999, p. 18.

The Character of Jesus

[6] Stefano di Giovanni, *The Agony in the Garden*, 1437, Detroit, Institute of Arts.

[7] Giovanni Bellini, *The Agony in the Garden,* 1465, London, National Gallery.

[8] Duccio di Buoninsegna, *Prayer on the Mount of Olives*, 1309, Siena, Museo dell opéra del Duomo.

⁹ Albrecht Dürer, *Christ on the Mount of Olives,* 1515, Vienna.

¹⁰ Rueland Frueauf the Elder, *The Agony in the Garden,* 1491, London, National Gallery.

¹¹ Albrecht Dürer, *Christ on the Mount of Olives,* 1521, Frankfurt, Städelsches Kunstinstitut.

¹² Anne-Francois-Louis Janmot, *Christ on the Mount of Olives,* 1840, Lyon, Musée des Beaux-Arts.

¹³ Hans Multscher, *Prayer on the Mount of Olives,* 1437, Berlin, Staatliche Museen.

¹⁴ Mark 14:35.

¹⁵ Ki-Chang Woonbo Kim, *Christ in Gethsemane,* 1952, Korea.

¹⁶ Jesus Mafa, *Christ on Gethsemane,* 1973, Cameroon.

¹⁷ Walter Richard West, *Gethsemane,* 1954, Oklahoma.

The Angel Who Offers the Cup or the Cross

¹⁸ Benvenuto di Giovanni, *The Agony in the Garden,* 1490, Washington, National Gallery.

[19] Andrea Mantegna, *The Agony in the Garden,* 1455, London, National Gallery.

[20] Lorenzo Ghiberti, *The Agony in the Garden,* 1440, Florence, Florence Cathedral.

[21] Théodore Chassériau, *Christ on the Mount of Olives*, 1840, Lyon, Musée des Beaux-arts.

[22] Sebastiano Ricci, *The Agony in the Garden,* 1730, Vienna, Kunsthistorisches Museum.

[23] William Blake, *The Agony in the Garden*, 1800, London, Tate Collections.

[24] Heinrich Hofman, *Christ in the Garden of Gethsemane,* 1890, New York, Riverside Church.

The Disciples

[25] Giovanni di Paolo, *The Agony in the Garden,* 1445, Vatican, Picture Gallery.

[26] Lo Spagna, *The Agony in the Garden,* 1500, London, National Gallery.

[27] Sandro Botticelli, *The Agony in the Garden,* 1500, Royal Chapel of Grenada.

[28] Andrea Mantegna, *The Agony in the Garden,* 1455, London, National Gallery.

[29] Giovanni Bellini, *The Agony in the Garden,* 1465, London, National Gallery.

[30] Albrecht Dürer, *The Large Passion*, 1496, Vienna.

The Garden

[31] Sandro Botticelli, *The Agony in the Garden*, 1500, Royal Chapel of Grenada.

[32] Giovanni Bellini, *The Agony in the Garden*, 1459, London, National Gallery.

[33] Fra Angelico, *The Agony in the Garden*, 1440, Florence, Convent of San Marco.

[34] Anne-Francois-Louis Janmot, *Christ on the Mount of Olives,* 1840, Lyon, Musée des Beaux-Arts.

[35] The expression is also known as *Mater dolorosa* and refers to the sorrowful Virgin represented in a seated position with her face deformed by pain and carrying in her arms the inert body of her son who has been taken down from the cross.

[36] James Tissot, *The Agony in the garden,* 1896, New York, Brooklyn Museum.

[37] Michel Feuillet, *Représenter Dieu,* Paris, DBB, 2007, p. 96.

Christ on the Mount of Olives by **Paul Gauguin**

[38] Set of late 19th and early 20th century artistic trends diverging from or opposing Impressionism (Neo-Impressionism, Synthetism, Nabis, prefigurations of Expressionism or Fauvism).

[39] Bernard Clavel, *Gauguin,* Lyon, 1958, p. 23.

[40] Ibid., p. 42.

[41] B. Clavel, *op. cit.,* p. 20.

[42] Norton Museum of Art, West Palm Beach, Florida.

[43] Paul Gauguin, Letter to Schuffenecker, October 8th, 1888.

[44] Alain Buisine, *Passion de Gauguin*, Paris, 2012, p. 172.

[45] Bernard Clavel, *op. cit.,* p. 35.

[46] Alain Buisine, *op.cit.,* p. 91.

The Agony in the Garden by **Rembrandt Van Rijn**

[47] Émile Michel, *Les chefs-d'œuvre de Rembrandt,* Paris, 1906, p. 86.

[48] Ibid., p. 54.

[49] Paul Baudiquey, *Un évangile selon Rembrandt,* Belgique, 1989, p. 37.

[50] Aquatint is a process of intaglio engraving on a metal plate using a chemical mordant (an acid).

[51] 11.1 x 8.4 cm.

[52] Paul Baudiquey, *Un évangile selon Rembrandt,* Belgique, 1989, p. 39.

[53] Blaise Pascal, *Thoughts II,* Paris, Gallimard, 1977, p. 32.

[54] Cited by Michael Bockemühl, Rembrandt: *The Mystery of the Revealed Form,* Cologne, 1992, p. 78.

[55] Paul Baudiquey, *op.cit.,* p. 24.

[56] Bernadette Neipp, *Gethsémané, Rembrandt et le dernier combat de Jésus,* Switzerland, 1999, p. 74.

[57] François Mauriac, *Life of Jesus,* Paris, 1936, p. 223.

[58] Bernadette Neipp, *op.cit.,* p. 74

[59] Picture Encyclopaedia, Art. Rembrandt, Paris, 1926, p. 62.

[60] Martine Vasselin, *Encyclopaedia Universalis,* corpus 20, Paris, 2011, p. 475.

[61] Bernadette Neipp, *Gethsémané, Rembrandt et le dernier combat de Jésus*, Switzerland, 1999, pp. 74-75.

Conclusion

[62] "Since my childhood misfortune has struck me. Never a chance, never a joy. Everything always against me and I cry out: my God, if you exist, I accuse you of injustice." Paul Gauguin, letter to William Molard, Tahiti, 1897.